Y0-BVQ-656

DO NOT REMOVE
CARDS FROM POCKET

THE PACIFIC ISLANDERS

The Peoples of North America

THE PACIFIC ISLANDERS

Douglas Ford

CHELSEA HOUSE PUBLISHERS

New York   Philadelphia

On the cover: A typically large Hawaiian family poses in front of a traditional
Polynesian dwelling in a photograph taken in the late 1800s.

CHELSEA HOUSE PUBLISHERS
Editor-in-Chief: Nancy Toff
Executive Editor: Remmel T. Nunn
Managing Editor: Karyn Gullen Browne
Copy Chief: Juliann Barbato
Picture Editor: Adrian G. Allen
Art Director: Maria Epes
Manufacturing Manager: Gerald Levine

The Peoples of North America
Senior Editor: Sean Dolan

Staff for THE PACIFIC ISLANDERS
Associate Editor: Abigail Meisel
Copy Editor: Phil Koslow
Deputy Copy Chief: Nicole Bowen
Editorial Assistant: Elizabeth Nix
Picture Research: PAR/NYC
Assistant Art Director: Loraine Machlin
Senior Designer: Noreen M. Lamb
Production Coordinator: Joseph Romano
Cover Illustration: Paul Biniasz
Banner Design: Hrana L. Janto

First Printing

1 3 5 7 9 8 6 4 2

Library of Congress Cataloging-in-Publication Data
Ford, Douglas, 1956–
    The Pacific islanders / Douglas Ford.
        p.   cm. —(The Peoples of North America)
    Bibliography: p.
    Includes index.
    Summary: Discusses the history, culture, and religion of the Pacific Islanders, factors
encouraging their emigration, and their acceptance as an ethnic group in North
America.
    ISBN 0-87754-883-8
        0-7910-0300-0 (pbk.)
    1. Oceanian Americans—Juvenile literature.   2. Islands of the Pacific—Civilization—
Juvenile Literature.   [1. Oceanian Americans.]   I. Title.   II. Series.   87-36977
E184.06F67 1988   CIP
973'.0499—dc19   AC

CONTENTS

THE PEOPLES OF NORTH AMERICA

CHELSEA HOUSE PUBLISHERS

A NATION
OF NATIONS

Daniel Patrick Moynihan

T he Constitution of the United States begins: "We the
People of the United States . . ." Yet, as we know, the
United States is not made up of a single group of peo-
ple. It is made up of many peoples. Immigrants from Europe,
Asia, Africa, and Central and South America settled in North
America seeking a new life filled with opportunities unavailable
in their homeland. Coming from many nations, they forged one
nation and made it their own. More than 100 years ago, Walt
Whitman expressed this perception of America as a melting pot:
"Here is not merely a nation, but a teeming Nation of nations."

Although the ingenuity and acts of courage of these immigrants, our ancestors, shaped the North American way of life, we
sometimes take their contributions for granted. This fine series,
The Peoples of North America, examines the experiences and contributions of the immigrants and how these contributions determined the future of the United States and Canada.

Immigrants did not abandon their ethnic traditions when they
reached the shores of North America. Each ethnic group had its
own customs and traditions, and each brought different experiences, accomplishments, skills, values, styles of dress, and tastes

in food that lingered long after its arrival. Yet this profusion of differences created a singularity, or bond, among the immigrants.

The United States and Canada are unusual in this respect. Whereas religious and ethnic differences have sparked intolerance throughout the rest of the world—from the 17th-century religious wars to the 19th-century nationalist movements in Europe to the near extermination of the Jewish people under Nazi Germany—North Americans have struggled to learn how to respect each other's differences and live in harmony.

Millions of immigrants from scores of homelands brought diversity to our continent. In a mass migration, some 12 million immigrants passed through the waiting rooms of New York's Ellis Island; thousands more came to the West Coast. At first, these immigrants were welcomed because labor was needed to meet the demands of the Industrial Age. Soon, however, the new immigrants faced the prejudice of earlier immigrants who saw them as a burden on the economy. Legislation was passed to limit immigration. The Chinese Exclusion Act of 1882 was among the first laws closing the doors to the promise of America. The Japanese were also effectively excluded by this law. In 1924, Congress set immigration quotas on a country-by-country basis.

Such prejudices might have triggered war, as they did in Europe, but North Americans chose negotiation and compromise instead. This determination to resolve differences peacefully has been the hallmark of the peoples of North America.

The remarkable ability of Americans to live together as one people was seriously threatened by the issue of slavery. It was a symptom of growing intolerance in the world. Thousands of settlers from the British Isles had arrived in the colonies as indentured servants, agreeing to work for a specified number of years on farms or as apprentices in return for passage to America and room and board. When the first Africans arrived in the then-British colonies during the 17th century, some colonists thought that they too should be treated as indentured servants. Eventually, the question of whether the Africans should be viewed as indentured, like the English, or as slaves who could be owned for life, was considered in a Maryland court. The court's calamitous decree held that blacks were slaves bound to lifelong servitude, and so were their children. America went through a time of moral examination and civil war before it finally freed African slaves and their descendants. The principle that all people are created equal had faced its greatest challenge and survived.

Yet the court ruling that set blacks apart from other races fanned flames of discrimination that burned long after slavery was abolished—and that still flicker today. The concept of racism had existed for centuries in countries throughout the world. For instance, when the Manchus conquered China in the 13th century, they decreed that Chinese and Manchus could not intermarry. To impress their superiority on the conquered Chinese, the Manchus ordered all Chinese men to wear their hair in a long braid called a queue.

By the 19th century, some intellectuals took up the banner of racism, citing Charles Darwin. Darwin's scientific studies hypothesized that highly evolved animals were dominant over other animals. Some advocates of this theory applied it to humans, asserting that certain races were more highly evolved than others and thus were superior.

This philosophy served as the basis for a new form of discrimination, not only against nonwhite people but also against various ethnic groups. Asians faced harsh discrimination and were depicted by popular 19th-century newspaper cartoonists as depraved, degenerate, and deficient in intelligence. When the Irish flooded American cities to escape the famine in Ireland, the cartoonists caricatured the typical "Paddy" (a common term for Irish immigrants) as an apelike creature with jutting jaw and sloping forehead.

By the 20th century, racism and ethnic prejudice had given rise to virulent theories of a Northern European master race. When Adolf Hitler came to power in Germany in 1933, he popularized the notion of Aryan supremacy. *Aryan*, a term referring to the Indo-European races, was applied to so-called superior physical characteristics such as blond hair, blue eyes, and delicate facial features. Anyone with darker and heavier features was considered inferior. Buttressed by these theories, the German Nazi state from

1933 to 1945 set out to destroy European Jews, along with Poles, Russians, and other groups considered inferior. It nearly succeeded. Millions of these people were exterminated.

The tragedies brought on by ethnic and racial intolerance throughout the world demonstrate the importance of North America's efforts to create a society free of prejudice and inequality.

A relatively recent example of the New World's desire to resolve ethnic friction nonviolently is the solution the Canadians found to a conflict between two ethnic groups. A long-standing dispute as to whether Canadian culture was properly English or French resurfaced in the mid-1960s, dividing the peoples of the French-speaking Quebec Province from those of the English-speaking provinces. Relations grew tense, then bitter, then violent. The Royal Commission on Bilingualism and Biculturalism was established to study the growing crisis and to propose measures to ease the tensions. As a result of the commission's recommendations, all official documents and statements from the national government's capital at Ottawa are now issued in both French and English, and bilingual education is encouraged.

The year 1980 marked a coming of age for the United States's ethnic heritage. For the first time, the U.S. Census asked people about their ethnic background. Americans chose from more than 100 groups, including French Basque, Spanish Basque, French Canadian, Afro-American, Peruvian, Armenian, Chinese, and Japanese. The ethnic group with the largest response was English (49.6 million). More than 100 million Americans claimed ancestors from the British Isles, which includes England, Ireland, Wales, and Scotland. There were almost as many Germans (49.2 million) as English. The Irish-American population (40.2 million) was third, but the next largest ethnic group, the Afro-Americans, was a distant fourth (21 million). There was a sizable group of French ancestry (13 million), as well as of Italian (12 million). Poles, Dutch, Swedes, Norwegians, and Russians followed. These groups, and other smaller ones, represent the wondrous profusion of ethnic influences in North America.

Canada, too, has learned more about the diversity of its population. Studies conducted during the French/English conflict showed that Canadians were descended from Ukrainians, Germans, Italians, Chinese, Japanese, native Indians, and Eskimos, among others. Canada found it had no ethnic majority, although nearly half of its immigrant population had come from the British Isles. Canada, like the United States, is a land of immigrants for whom mutual tolerance is a matter of reason as well as principle.

The people of North America are the descendants of one of the greatest migrations in history. And that migration is not over. Koreans, Vietnamese, Nicaraguans, Cubans, and many others are heading for the shores of North America in large numbers. This mix of cultures shapes every aspect of our lives. To understand ourselves, we must know something about our diverse ethnic ancestry. Nothing so defines the North American nations as the motto on the Great Seal of the United States: *E Pluribus Unum*— Out of Many, One.

Hawaii officially became a U.S. territory in 1900. This photograph, taken from the deck of the USS Boston, *captures a moment during the annexation ceremonies.*

THE PACIFIC: PAST, PRESENT, AND FUTURE

The story of Pacific Islanders in the United States differs from that of nearly every other ethnic group in America. Most immigrants traveled across vast distances to reach U.S. shores, making the journey without any guarantee of entry through the "golden door." Those who obtained permission to remain in America first had to secure employment and then endure a wait of five years before becoming eligible to apply for U.S. citizenship.

In contrast, Pacific Islanders found themselves in possession of many—if not all—of the rights and privileges of American citizens before even setting foot outside their homeland. They had no need to travel to the United States, because the U.S. government was already a fixture on many of the thousands of small islands located in the Pacific. Some island kingdoms, such as Hawaii, had been appropriated as colonies by the United States. Others, such as Guam, had been spoils of war wrested by the United States from foreign powers. Still others fell into U.S. control after World War II, when they were declared U.S. trust territories by the United Nations.

The incursion of the United States into the Pacific began in the 19th century, when whaling vessels from New England found safe haven in the natural harbors of the easternmost islands of Polynesia—a group known then as the Sandwich Islands and today as Hawaii. The sailors from these ships were soon followed by Christian missionaries. These preachers and their families in turn paved the way for plantation owners and other American business interests, which came increasingly to dominate the islands' economy and government. By 1900 all eight Hawaiian islands had become a U.S. territory.

In 1898 the United States expanded its influence in the Pacific by acquiring territory in Micronesia, another of the Pacific's three major island groups. Originally a colonial possession of Spain, the Micronesian island of Guam passed into the domain of the United States after the Spanish-American War. For nearly 50 years Guam remained the only American holding in the region. But after World War II, the United States gained control of all of Micronesia when the United Nations declared it a U.S. trust territory. Thus, the United States entered the postwar era with strongholds in both Micronesia and Polynesia. The third Pacific region—Melanesia—continued to be independent of American influence and has never sent a significant number of emigrants to U.S. shores. Almost all Pacific Islanders in the United States trace their origin to Micronesia and Polynesia.

It is only since the 1950s that great numbers of Pacific Islanders have left Micronesia and Polynesia for the United States. Their immigration has been spurred by a desire for education, employment, and health care not available on the islands. But the greatest impetus to immigration has been the rapid increase in the Pacific islands' population, which almost doubled in the 20 years between 1960 and 1980. This sudden growth has put an added strain on every available resource, from housing and water to employment and medical care.

As the population grows, so too does the islanders' desire for a better quality of life. Local governments in Micronesia and Polynesia have often found it difficult to satisfy demands for jobs, schools, and hospitals, especially in rural areas. Therefore, increasing numbers of Pacific Islanders have sought a better life in urban centers such as Pago Pago, located in American

In 1987, residents of Belau, an island in Micronesia's Caroline group, voted to adopt the Compact of Free Association with the United States. After years of foreign domination, Micronesians are becoming increasingly outspoken in demanding self-determination.

Samoa. The migration from countryside to city has so shifted the foundations of the islands' agrarian societies that the great exodus of Pacific Islanders to the United States seems far less drastic than it might have otherwise.

Once in America, Pacific Islanders found employment in Hawaii and in the cities of the West Coast, where the majority of them settled. Many worked as enlisted personnel or civilian employees on naval bases. In general, men have tended to seek jobs at ports of entry, such as airports or docks, whereas women have worked in hotels, hospitals, nursing homes, and the fish canneries of the Pacific Northwest. A very small number of Pacific Islanders have joined the white-collar sector of the work force. Although about 25 to 30 percent of all Polynesian and Micronesian immigrants failed to secure any permanent jobs in America, they were nevertheless better off than they had been at home, where fierce competition for employment made their chances even worse.

And unlike many of their American contemporaries, Pacific Islanders know that in times of hardship

In 1983, Rear Admiral Bruce DeMars (to left of speaker, in white uniform and cap), commander of the U.S. naval forces in the Mariana Islands, attended the graduation ceremonies at Outer Islands High School on one of the islands of Ulithi, an atoll group located near Guam. The U.S. Navy has been a constant presence in Guam since the end of the Spanish-American War in 1898.

they can rely on an extended community network of friends and family. In Samoan, Tongan, and Guamanian neighborhoods, newcomers to the United States receive shelter, food, and money from members of their immediate and extended families. Often in these districts, four generations live together under a single roof, where both English and a native tongue—be it Tongan, Samoan, or Chamorro (the language of many Guamanians)—can be heard. Pacific Islanders find support, too, in the many churches that dot their neighborhoods. Congregants come together to celebrate national and religious holidays and to reaffirm their identity as people of the Pacific islands.

Today, approximately 100,000 Pacific Islanders call the United States their home. For many the transition from their native land to their adopted one has been smooth. For others, the struggle to establish an identity in the United States has proven frustrating because the vast majority of Americans have lumped Pacific Islanders together with myriad other ethnic groups, most often Asians. Despite these obstacles, Pacific Islanders continue to migrate to urban centers in all 50 states, but the vast majority flock to San Diego, San Francisco, and other cities on the West Coast. As their numbers grow, they will undoubtedly win greater admiration for their ancient heritage and for the devotion to church and family that sustains them in their new home.

Natives of the Solomon Islands
disembark from war canoes, circa 1922.

THE ERA OF GREAT VOYAGES

Approximately 25,000 years ago, during the Ice Age, a series of great migrations by the inhabitants of southern China and Southeast Asia began. The population of entire villages set out into the vast Pacific in double-hulled canoes, some with sails, in search of new homes in the islands to the south and the east. Navigating without the benefit of modern instruments such as the compass, these ancient mariners plotted their course by studying the position of the stars, the direction of the wind and waves, and the shapes of clouds. The voyagers also found land by following the migratory patterns of birds. The first travelers to leave their Asian homeland ended their journey on the continent of Australia and on the Pacific archipelago known as Melanesia, which means "black islands" and is located just west of Indonesia. Melanesia comprises New Guinea, the Solomon Islands, the New Hebrides Islands (today known as the Vanuatu Islands), Fiji, and numerous smaller islands.

A later group of voyagers began setting out across the Pacific in about 3000 B.C. These migrants first moved south into the islands now known as the Philippines and Indonesia and then headed for Polynesia (many islands) in huge canoes outfitted with sails. They landed first in Samoa and the Society Islands and later moved on to Hawaii, Easter Island, New Zealand, Phoenix Island, Tonga, the Cook Islands, and Tuvalu. Well before the year A.D. 1000, the furthest corners of

Polynesia—which lies within a roughly triangular perimeter, bordered by Hawaii to the north, Easter Island to the east, and New Zealand to the south—had been settled. The third important Pacific archipelago, Micronesia (small islands), lies mostly north of the equator, between Polynesia and the Philippines. Micronesia appears to have been settled by a combination of northward migration from Melanesia and Polynesia and eastward migration from Indonesia and the Philippines. Collectively, the three island groups settled by the seafarers from the Asian continent—Melanesia, Polynesia, and Micronesia—are known as Oceania. Oceania's thousands of islands are spread out over an area equal to more than one-third the size of the Pacific Ocean.

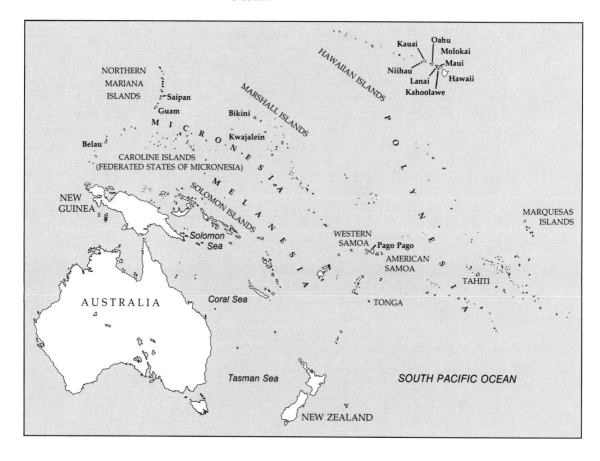

The Island Environment

Before their great migrations, most of the people who would populate Oceania were hunters and gatherers. But by about 3000 B.C. the new inhabitants of Polynesia and Melanesia were planting and harvesting their own crops and breeding domesticated animals. Because the islands the seafarers discovered on their journeys did not contain the variety of plants and animals necessary to sustain human life, the travelers brought with them everything they needed to survive, including seeds to plant crops, livestock, provisions, and tools and implements. The voyagers encountered two basic types of island—volcanic islands and atolls, which are coral islands consisting of a reef surrounding a lagoon. Volcanic islands usually offered both fresh water and fertile land, but atolls were usually less hospitable to newcomers. Most featured poor soil and lacked fresh water. Although the settlers toiled to develop the top-soil on the atolls, most saw their work ruined by the severe storms that frequently buffeted the small islands.

In 1913, native Hawaiians participated in a festival celebrating traditional Polynesian culture held near Honolulu.

Pacific Islanders traveled from island to island in canoes that they often outfitted with sails. Vessels similar to but larger than these were used to transport food supplies, plants, and even animals to uninhabited islands that the travelers wished to settle.

On more welcoming isles, the newcomers radically changed their environment by introducing foreign plants such as the banana, breadfruit, coconut, sweet potato, and yam. They also brought new species of animals with them, including pigs, dogs, chickens, and rats (the last came as stowaways on the voyagers' boats). Their new tropical homes proved unsuitable for the cultivation of rice, which had been the staple crop on the Asian mainland, so the islanders instead grew taro, an edible plant. When steamed for many hours, the taro plant's stem can be pounded into a highly nutritious food called *poi*. This versatile foodstuff could be dried and eaten during ocean voyages or stored underground for many years as a buffer against famine. It was so nutritious that people could survive on *poi* alone for many months. As might be expected, the island dwellers also depended on the ocean as a source of food and became skilled at fishing.

Life on the large volcanic islands proved easier than life on the atolls, and the islanders there often found themselves with a surplus of food. The additional food meant that the inhabitants of these more fertile lands could devote more time to activities other than fishing and farming. The most privileged natives of the large islands, the chiefs, collected tribute in the form of food and never had to worry about going hungry. In contrast, chiefs on atolls probably had to fish and cultivate land like everyone else in the community.

Island Society

Traditional Polynesian and Micronesian societies were generally divided into three classes: commoners, priests and craftsmen, and chiefs. On the larger islands, the commoners worked the land and fished in order to provide the food on which all of the classes survived. They also made textiles, such as woven mats, and fashioned cloth from the bark of the mulberry tree. Priests and craftsmen formed the middle level of society. It was the priests' job to keep track of genealogies and to make sure that rituals were observed. Craftsmen specialized in skills such as the hollowing out of logs to make canoes known as dugouts.

A rigid class system in which the chief was the single most important individual characterized both Polynesian and Micronesian societies. This drawing of the interior of a Hawaiian chief's dwelling was the work of Louis Choris, an artist who visited Hawaii with the Russian explorer Otto von Kotzebue in 1816.

Also grouped in the middle level of society were the lesser chiefs, who were regional representatives of a higher chief.

In some island societies it was possible to move between classes, but in general a person inherited his class from parents and grandparents. In some places the class system also included slaves (usually captured in war) or a caste of "unclean" people who were reviled by all others in their society. Both of these social standings were inherited by succeeding generations. In Polynesia, inheritance and genealogy were *patrilineal*, that is, traced through the father's family, and the firstborn son carried on the family name. Chiefs, for example, were usually the first son of a first son in a long line of island rulers. Micronesian society tended to be *matrilineal*. A man entered his wife's family through marriage, and the mother's land was passed through her daughters from generation to generation. Yet even within the matrilineal system, the eldest male or the eldest sister's son was usually in charge.

An engraving shows Samuel Wallis—commander of the first European expedition to Tahiti—greeting Purea, a Tahitian noblewoman. Accounts of Tahitian customs and culture had a profound effect on the European imagination. According to historian J. C. Beaglehole, "Wallis had stumbled on a foundation stone of the Romantic Movement."

The Chiefs

The chief's main function was to preside over ceremonies and to govern the community. He organized
community projects—the construction of irrigation
systems, for example—and used his power of tribute
to provide food and materials for the workers. Chiefs
on larger islands were very powerful. Generally a large
island was divided into wedges, like a pie, so that each
of the chiefs had a range of land from beachfront to
mountain range. Within such a realm, a chief exercised
absolute control over the lives of his people and the
use of the land. On smaller islands, where the chief
was not so powerful, the land was owned by the community. A chief's authority was based on the general
belief that he possessed *mana*, or spiritual power.
Mana was feared by those who did not wield it. Like
the title of *chief* itself, this power was passed down
through generations.

Warfare between neighboring chiefs was common
and usually was triggered by disputes over land. Some
scholars speculate that war was the primary force behind the migration of islanders throughout the Pacific.
According to this theory, defeated chieftains took to
the sea with their followers to discover and settle new
islands. This was especially true of ambitious younger
chiefs who stood little chance of toppling more expe-
rienced leaders. Over generations, the story of the migrations passed into the realm of legend, and the
voyager-chiefs assumed the status of gods in the eyes
of their people.

The Coming of the Europeans

It was during the 16th century that European explorers
first sailed the Pacific in search of a western sea route
to China, India, and Indonesia. In Europe, these lands
were believed to be fabulously wealthy and were
known as Cathay, the Indies, and the Spice Islands.
During the early 1500s, Portuguese navigator Ferdi-
nand Magellan hoisted the flag of his sponsor, King
Charles I of Spain, over many of the islands within
Micronesia. Magellan and his contemporaries encoun-

Because the first European explorers of Polynesia were more concerned with science than with colonization, they were careful to document the rites and rituals of Pacific culture. An engraving by John Webber, an artist who traveled with Captain Cook on his third and last voyage, depicts a kava-drinking *ceremony in Tonga. Over the following decades, many aspects of traditional Polynesian culture vanished as contact with whites increased.*

tered people of a common origin whose cultures had diverged during centuries of isolation. In fact, according to written accounts of the day, the explorers heard as many as 17 different languages.

For nearly 300 years following this initial contact, Europeans remained relatively uninterested in the smaller islands of the South Pacific, which did not seem to offer the same lucrative trade opportunities as India or China. Until the 19th century the culture of the Pacific Islanders underwent few changes as a result of contact with Europeans, but during the 1800s large numbers of white men—mostly whalers and missionaries—arrived in the South Pacific. The majority of whalers hailed from the United States and stopped in the Pacific Islands to replenish their stores of food and fresh water. Intent on converting the islanders to Christianity, the missionaries, most of them of American, English, or French origin, left an even greater mark on Oceania than did the whalers. Although missionaries and whalers saw each other as destructive influences on the islanders' way of life, both groups bore responsibility for permanently altering the Pacific Islands.

The whalers who began putting into port in Micronesia, Melanesia, and Polynesia in the early 1800s brought with them many items to trade for fresh food and water. Although the islanders found such items as sharp-edged tools, cloth, and firearms extremely useful and desirable, the introduction of foreign-made goods into the island economies profoundly affected the way of life there. Islanders began to depend on manufactured goods brought via ship from North America or Europe and ceased to practice the traditional crafts that had once provided them with building supplies, work implements, weapons, and clothing. The influx of new supplies and weapons further disrupted life on the islands by creating a gap between classes based solely on material wealth. For the first time there emerged a group of kings in Oceania who owed their authority not to noble lineage or mana but to the amount of material possessions they had been able to amass.

Whites brought not only manufactured goods but a less desirable import—a new set of infectious diseases. For the first time in their history, islanders were exposed to such contagions as measles and European and American strains of influenza. As the islanders lacked natural immunity to such scourges, the illnesses almost always proved deadly. Thousands fell to these plagues—and to venereal disease—which drastically reduced the overall population of the islands.

Christian missionaries arrived in Oceania at approximately the same time as the whalers. They greatly improved the quality of medical care, introduced modern educational methods to the islands, and took steps to preserve certain aspects of island culture, such as devising a written language from the islanders' spoken tongue. In other instances the missionaries were interested less in preserving than in eradicating elements of the indigenous culture they found in Oceania. Although the missionaries had little trouble in convincing the islanders to profess allegiance to Christianity, the converts also tended to hold on to their traditional religious beliefs. The Christian clerics were appalled by the custom of human sacrifice, which some islanders practiced in order to appease their angry gods, and the missionaries were no more pleased by the practice of cannibalism, which they encountered in the Marquesas and other islands. The more doctrinaire among them also had a hard time accepting that the purportedly converted islanders still wished to pray to their many deities, among whom were the personified spirits of natural forces and the souls of departed ancestors. The missionaries struggled not only against the recalcitrant islanders and what they perceived as the pernicious and amoral influence of the whalers but also against their colleagues from competing denominations. It was not unheard of for missionaries to conspire with island chiefs to have their fellow Christians expelled from the Pacific. This religious rivalry often grew extremely fierce. In one instance, French Catholic priests based in Hawaii required the protection of warships to defend them from the harassment of New

A British missionary preaches the Christian gospel to Hawaiians in this engraving by William Ellis, who sailed with Cook on his last voyage. By inculcating Western values, missionaries did much to aid the process of American and European colonization of the Pacific.

Captain James Cook, as portrayed in an engraving done in 1837. Sailing the same sort of flat-bottomed ship used to transport coal in the North Sea regions where he had been raised, Cook circumnavigated the world twice and charted the Pacific from the west coast of the Americas to the Arctic regions, Russia, Japan, Southeast Asia, Antarctica, and Oceania.

England Protestant proselytizers in the region. Sometimes this competition entangled missionaries in fighting between warring factions on an island.

As missionaries, traders, and whalers returned to their homelands, Oceania began to cast its own influence over the nations of Europe and North America. Captain James Cook, an English seaman who explored a number of Pacific islands, brought several artists with him on his voyages in the 1760s and 1770s. Their thousands of beautiful and detailed drawings and paintings excited the imagination of Europeans eager for news of the exotic discoveries in the South Pacific. The islands' strange flora and fauna, their tropical setting, the seeming innocence and unworldliness of their inhabitants, and the natives' handsome appearance and purportedly carefree and languorous existence all seemed to suggest paradise to the Europeans. Indeed, to much of Europe's literary and artistic community, the reports from Hawaii, Tahiti, and other idyllic isles seemed to confirm the notion of the so-called noble savage, as espoused by the influential French writer and philosopher Jean-Jacques Rousseau. According to Rousseau and others, man was naturally good and became corrupted only upon contact with the impure institutions of civilization. When a British sea captain brought a Pacific Islander named Omai to England in 1776, the Tahitian became the darling of London literary society and was even wined and dined by the esteemed biographer and man of letters James Boswell, who found him "elegant." This fascination only grew as contact between whites and Pacific Islanders increased in the 1800s. In *Typee*, published in 1846 and based on his actual experiences as a seaman attached to the New England whaler *Acushnet*, the great American novelist Herman Melville undermined the notion of the noble savage and explored the theme of evil in paradise, in the context of the practice of cannibalism by the otherwise peaceable native inhabitants of the Marquesas. European intoxication with the exoticism of the South Seas perhaps reached its artistic culmination in the brightly colored paintings of Paul Gauguin, who abandoned France for Tahiti and the Marquesas in 1891. But to his dismay, Gauguin discovered that Oceania had already been irrevocably altered by outside contact. Tahiti was under the administration of French colonial bureaucrats, and Gauguin had to flee to the interior to escape their officiousness. The painter had hoped to draw inspiration from native artifacts, including wooden tools, totems, and idols, but these products of the indigenous island culture were nonexistent, and Gauguin had to carve his own.

For all their exultation about the Pacific Islanders' nobility, Europeans and Americans did not forget that by their standards the natives were still essentially savages, uncivilized and ripe for colonization and economic exploitation. The Pacific islands were not neglected in the scramble among the world powers for

Woman of Tahiti, *by the French artist Paul Gauguin, whose visits to Tahiti and the Marquesas fired his artistic imagination.*

colonies and commerce and by 1900 had been divided among various European nations and the United States. Britain claimed Fiji, the Solomon Islands, Tonga, the Cook Islands, and other territories. France controlled the New Hebrides, New Caledonia, and French Polynesia. The United States flew its flag over

During the 1980s more than half the population of Micronesia migrated to urban centers, where they subsisted in squalid slums such as this one in Pohnpei. The rates of alcoholism, malnutrition, leprosy, suicide, and other blights are extremely high in such areas.

Hawaii, Guam, and Eastern Samoa, and Germany established colonies in Western Samoa and in the Mariana, Caroline, and Marshall islands. During the 20th century the political status of the islands of Oceania has varied, usually in response to fluctuations in the balance of power between the European nations, Japan, and the United States.

The Challenge to Tradition

Through two centuries of change, some aspects of island life and tradition have endured. Most people feel strong bonds to family and community, particularly on the more rural islands. This link between an individual and the larger society echoes the values of an earlier time, when the community's survival depended on people working together. Many islanders are taught from earliest childhood not to be competitive or confrontational and to share with others who are in need. This humanistic creed sometimes impedes islanders when they are faced with the harsher environment of larger cities in the Pacific or on the U.S. mainland.

Nevertheless, Pacific Islanders are moving in great numbers to cities within their island groups and in the United States and New Zealand. In almost every case, the motivation behind emigration is to seek better economic opportunity.

Indeed, islanders first began immigrating to the U.S. mainland to share in the wealth of the California gold rush in 1849. News of the find had raced through

The poverty of Micronesia is evident in this scarred graveyard in Ebeye, on the Marshall Islands atoll of Kwajalein.

In the 20th century, ties between the United States and Oceania have grown stronger. American influence is particularly strong in such areas as Pago Pago, the capital of American Samoa, where television sets are used as audiovisual aids at the Olomoana Elementary School.

the Pacific, where it had the same effect as it did everywhere else—people flocked to California in search of gold. The West Coast is still the focal point of settlement for Pacific Islander immigrants, who have been coming to the United States in increasing numbers since the 1950s. In the 1980s, over half of the Americans who claim Pacific ancestry live in Hawaii. Two-thirds of the remainder reside in Alaska, California, Oregon, and Washington, according to the 1980 U.S. census. All told, there are some 100,000 Pacific Islanders living in the United States.

Although resettlement in the United States has eased many of the economic hardships faced by Pacific Islanders, migration has ushered in a new set of prob-

lems. In America the islanders are often confused with one another and with other, more prevalent minority groups. To preserve their island heritage and to provide support on the mainland, many have established community organizations in the hope of easing the transition from the homeland of their ancestors to their adopted country.

Although some Micronesians have benefited from improved health care and education in the postwar period, many have suffered from a deteriorating standard of living. Residents of Kwajalein Atoll, in the Marshall Islands, have few advantages to offer their children, shown here playing in a garbage dump.

This 1905 photograph shows Hawaiian fishermen using nets and spears to capture their prey.

HAWAII: TRADITION CHALLENGED

The first inhabitants of the Hawaiian islands arrived there about A.D. 600. They came from the east, from the Marquesas, and quickly settled the eight major islands of Hawaii—Kahoolawe, Kauai, Lanai, Maui, Molokai, Niihau, Oahu, and Hawaii, which is the largest of the islands. The traditions they practiced in their new homeland dated back almost 2,000 years.

The culture of the Hawaiian islands was very similar to that of the other large island communities. The Hawaiians led highly structured lives, guided by an elaborate system of taboos called *kapu*. Those taboos applying to women were particularly rigorous. Women ate separately from men and were not allowed to eat pork, bananas, and turtle meat. Women's food had to be cooked in a separate oven. They were not allowed to cultivate taro, and they produced only crops of lesser importance.

The three major social classes—commoners, priests, and the ruling class—were segregated much more strictly than were men and women. Although it shared an ancestry with the community at large, the ruling class avoided contact with the commoners, maintaining strict class distinctions through the kapu system. A commoner who violated kapu—for example, by failing to show the proper respect to a member of the ruling class—was subject to severe penalties, including death. Babies of mixed blood were slain so that the upper caste's bloodline would not be tainted. Brothers and sisters of the ruling class sometimes married in order to preserve the purity of a family's lineage. Whites would later cite infanticide and incest as proof that Hawaiians were immoral heathens, when in fact the Hawaiian people were following their own highly developed moral code.

Although antagonism ran high between classes, a feeling of closeness bound members of the same class. Commoners freely shared their material goods and helped one another with such tasks as building a house or clearing large tracts of land. Generosity within the community often extended to such primary responsibilities as the rearing of offspring. Orphaned children found new homes under the roof of a friend or neighbor. Because the typical Hawaiian extended family tended to include many members, the addition of one or two adopted children rarely seemed a burden. Foreign visitors frequently commented on the Hawaiians' great love of children.

An 1857 etching shows Hawaiians congregating at Honolulu Beach on the island of Oahu. Hawaiian villagers generally enjoyed a tight-knit community life.

The warm relationship between children and adults was mirrored in the feelings of the people for their chief. Although he invariably belonged to the ruling class, the chief held no contempt for the commoners, whom he regarded with respect and concern. The strong bond between the leader and his people proved vital during wartime. Hawaiians usually indulged in warfare for two reasons: to win territory or to avenge the death of an important member of a village. Only chiefs possessed the authority to declare wars, which they fought either against other local chiefs or rulers of distant islands. As most chiefs had the ambition of ruling all eight Hawaiian islands themselves, there was ample ground for rivalry and competition among the various potentates.

All adult males, regardless of class, were expected to be warriors. Hawaiians received no real military training, but they did play many competitive games, which sharpened their fighting skills and conditioned them for endurance during battles. During these tournaments, men demonstrated their mastery of the javelin and other weapons, including daggers, slings, and long cords used for strangling. But most battles consisted of hand-to-hand combat in which the warring parties struck each other with fists or short clubs.

The Hawaiians enjoyed a spiritual life if not always a peaceful one. They worshiped many gods and held great celebratory feasts called *luaus*, the most important of which, Makahiki, honored the god Lono. According to legend, while still a mortal Lono had killed his wife in a fit of rage. After wandering the islands in a state of grief, he set out to sea in a strange craft, never to be seen again, although Hawaiians believed that one day he would return to them. War was kapu at this time of great feasting and celebration. The many activities included *hulas*, a combination of prayer and dance, which were offered to the high chief and to the gods. There were also athletic events such as surfing, invented by the Hawaiians, and a sport, engaged in only by the chiefs, which consisted of riding a sled down a chute lined with smooth stones. It was during this most important of festivals that Captain James Cook first sighted the islands.

William Ellis drew this scene of hula dancers performing at a luau, *or celebratory feast, in 1823.*

Captain Cook in Hawaii

Cook spotted the Hawaiian islands on January 18, 1778. Notwithstanding that the islands were already inhabited, Cook credited himself as a discoverer, like Columbus, Magellan, and other European explorers before him. He called his find the Sandwich Islands, in honor of England's earl of Sandwich, Cook's friend and patron and the head of the British Admiralty. For many years Hawaii was widely known as the Sandwich Islands.

Cook visited the islands three times, twice during Lono's festival. He was a great admirer of the Hawaiians' seafaring skills and other elements of their culture, and his knowledge of Tahitian made it surprisingly easy for him to learn Hawaiian. The Hawaiians also held Cook in high regard, and after his second arrival during Makahiki they deified him, believing him to be the reincarnation of Lono. This visit lasted three months. The British set sail for home in early February 1779 but were forced to return to the islands after six days in order to make repairs to a damaged mast. There, they found the islanders much changed in their attitudes. Apparently, the sudden return of the ships—gods were expected to appear only at long intervals—had convinced the islanders that Cook was not divine. In spite of his best efforts, Cook could not control his crew, which broke a variety of kapus, behaved ungallantly with the island women, and killed a Hawaiian. On February 13, 1779, Cook was stabbed and then beaten to death by a group of islanders in a dispute over a dinghy belonging to his boat, the *Discovery*. His carcass was hacked to pieces and his flesh burned, but the Hawaiians preserved some of his bones, as they did for their own great chieftains. When the English demanded that Cook's remains be turned over to them for burial, they were presented with part of his femur, which the crew then committed to the sea in a traditional sailor's funeral.

In important ways, Cook's visits foreshadowed the events of the next century in Hawaii. Cook understood the importance of the islands as a way station for Pacific voyages, and he established a pattern of trade—swapping manufactured goods for provisions—that was continued by the whalers who began calling at Hawaii in the 1800s. His death illustrated the ways in which even the best-intentioned contacts between whites and islanders could be rendered perilous for both groups by cultural misunderstanding.

A New Age of Warfare

The effect Cook had on Hawaiians did not end with his death. Prior to his visits, none of the four separate kingdoms in the islands had been able to score a decisive victory over the others using traditional methods, but Cook and his men introduced a new element of warfare—guns. The kingdoms Cook and later visi-

In July 1777, Captain Cook arrived in Tangatapu, an island group south of Tonga. Cook explored the islands with British landscape painter John Webber, who sketched a traditional ceremony celebrating the entrance into adulthood of Tangatapu's king. The drawing won the admiration of French artist R. Benard, who used it as a basis for the engraving shown here.

tors came in contact with also learned how to profit by mastering the strategy of trading provisions. They became accustomed to dealing with foreign visitors and used their diplomatic skills to gain the support of these newcomers for their cause. One chief, Kamehameha I, whose name is usually translated into English as The One Set Apart, surpassed all others in effectively combining this newfound skill with traditional methods of warfare.

Kamehameha I has become a legendary figure in Hawaiian history. The story of his birth is given in *Hawaii and Its People* by historian A. Grove Day.

On a November night of storm—the year is not known, but 1758 is a good guess, for the portentous star that blazed at the birth was probably Halley's comet—a son was born to Kekuiapoiwa. The soothsayers of Alapai had reported that the

Renowned as a great warrior, King Kamehameha I fends off spears hurled at him during a mock battle. The Hawaiians participated in many exercises and games designed to hone their fighting skills.

baby would be a rebel who would "slay the chiefs." The king therefore gave orders, Herod-like, that the child should be killed as soon as it was born. The mother had made a plan, however, and at birth the little chief was spirited away by a man named Naeole and reared in the mountains by foster parents.

Kamehameha I was brought back into the royal court five years later, raised as a prince, and taught the art of war. He grew into a powerful warrior who proved himself in battle by winning many bloody conflicts for his home island of Hawaii. By 1779, the year of Cook's arrival, Kamehameha I had earned a place as one of the most prominent warriors in the army of his uncle Kalaniopuu, the king of western Hawaii. In fact, many believe that Kamehameha I and Cook first met while sailing in the offshore waters of Hawaii. According to one account of this historic encounter, Kamehameha I was then returning from an unsuccessful assault on the island of Maui and directed Cook to a nearby harbor called the Road of the Gods.

In 1791, Kamehameha I succeeded his uncle as ruler of western Hawaii and went on to win control of other islands in the chain, a feat requiring an army of 16,000 warriors, many armed with European firearms. As guardian of the temple of the war god, Kamehameha I paid the deity homage in both ritual and deed. During one battle, called the Damming of the Waters, the bodies of fallen warriors were stacked so high that they blocked the Iao River. To his countrymen, it seemed that Kamehameha I had been singled out for special favor by the gods, particularly after a battle on the Big Island (Hawaii) during which the volcano Kilauea erupted suddenly and killed hundreds of his opponents. In 1810, Kamehameha I finally unified all eight of the Hawaiian islands.

From Warrior to Statesman

As king, Kamehameha I assembled a distinguished group of nearly 50 European and American advisers. Two of the first, the Englishmen John Young and Isaac

This portrait of Kamehameha I in 1816, at age 58, was copied by an unknown artist from a painting by Louis Choris. Choris portrayed the king in both European and traditional Hawaiian dress; Kamehameha preferred this version.

Davis, established a close tie between Britain and Hawaii. In 1794, Kamehameha I declared the islands a part of England, although this act was never recognized by the British government. Although Kamehameha relied heavily on his foreign consultants, his kingdom did not fall into the control of outsiders because he never let his European and American aides forget that he commanded a formidable army, capable of quickly crushing an invasion from abroad.

Kamehameha I attracted the attention of world powers because Hawaii was an important supply station for Asia-bound trade ships, but the king envisioned an even greater future for his nation and dreamed of building a Pacific monarchy that rivaled the most splendid courts of Europe. He realized that in order to develop its economy Hawaii needed an export item. After toying with several possibilities, he settled upon the fragrant yellow heartwood of the sandalwood tree as the ideal commodity. Sandalwood commanded a high price throughout the Orient, where it was used as incense and as the material from which artisans carved ornamental cabinetwork and religious objects. The king declared a royal monopoly on the valuable tree.

Kamehameha's scheme succeeded so well that for years after his death in 1819, Hawaii's royalty relied almost solely on sandalwood for its sizable income. The islands' aristocracy made unreasonable demands on the common people to supply the profitable wood, which grew scarcer each year. As a result of this burden, commoners neglected their crops, and the islanders' health declined as a result of having to work day and night in the wet upland forests where sandalwood grew. Many died of disease and exhaustion. In the

After the death of Kamehameha I in 1819, his prime minister, High Chief Kalanimoku, requested baptism from a French expedition sailing through the Hawaiian islands. On August 13, 1819, his request was granted, and the abbé de Quélen performed the ceremony aboard the L'Uranie.

end, the tree virtually disappeared from the islands, and the profit from its sale failed to pay the enormous debt incurred by the ruling class.

Whalers and Missionaries

During the 19th century, whale oil lubricated the machines and lit the homes of North America, and whaling vessels roamed the Pacific in search of their prey. The first whaler entered Hawaiian waters in 1819. By the 1840s hundreds of these ships and their crews were calling at Hawaiian ports each year. The islands profited through port taxes and through the establishment of businesses—such as warehouses and bars—that sprang up to serve the trade and its practitioners. Like the commerce in sandalwood, the whaling industry was also doomed to a short life. With the discovery of

Harpoonists in a longboat move in for the kill on a sperm whale in the waters off Hawaii. The islands became a popular port of call for whalers during the 19th century.

petroleum in the early 1870s, whaling's importance diminished. It was not long before petroleum replaced whale oil as the primary fuel in America.

Although whaling brought a good deal of money to Hawaii, it also disrupted the life of the islands. Sailors on board commercial vessels, most of whom had been away from land for some time, counted on satisfying their thirst for drink and their desire for women in Hawaii. In doing so, the seamen raised the ire of a well-organized opposition force—the missionaries.

In early 1820, Hawaii's first missionaries—a contingent from Boston composed of seven Protestant families and four Hawaiians, all led by the Reverend Hiram Bingham—landed on the islands. These Christians from America could not have chosen a better mo-

Whalers and merchant ships often sought safe haven in Honolulu Harbor, photographed here in 1856. By the mid-19th century hundreds of these ships and their crews were using Hawaiian ports each year.

ment to arrive. Liholiho, Kamehameha's successor, had abolished the traditional Hawaiian religion, which he regarded as too restrictive, just months before. The king granted the missionaries a one-year stay on a trial basis. He asked them to begin their work by educating the ruling class in reading and writing. At the end of the first year the missionaries had succeeded in bringing the island's tribal nobility to literacy, thus earning themselves a welcome of indefinite length.

Although they replaced many native customs with Christian ones, the missionaries took some pains to preserve traditional Hawaiian culture. For example, they declined merely to teach Hawaiians to speak, read, and write English. Instead, they transcribed Hawaiian using an alphabet of 12 letters (*a, e, h, i, k, l, m, n, o, p, u,* and *w*) that corresponded to the sounds in spoken Hawaiian. This system was used to translate the Bible and other works. By the mid-1800s almost the entire population of the islands had achieved literacy.

The missionaries' efforts were so successful that by 1863 the American board overseeing their work considered their mission complete. Hawaii then became a base for further missions into other areas of the Pacific. Although it cannot be denied that in suppressing the remnants of Hawaii's traditional religion the missionaries helped destroy a vital part of the islanders' identity, the American clerics preserved the Hawaiian language in a written form and introduced social controls that saved the Hawaiian people from possible destruction by alcohol and venereal disease.

The Decline of a Kingdom

The 19th century was a bleak time for Hawaiians. At the time of Captain Cook's arrival an estimated 300,000 native dwellers inhabited the Hawaiian islands, but by 1910 only 38,547 remained, and that figure included those with only partial Hawaiian ancestry. By 1960 the native population had dwindled to 10,502, according to the U.S. Census Bureau. Each group that shaped Hawaii's history—primarily the English and the Americans—bears some of the responsibility for the population's decline.

(continued on page 57)

Overleaf: King William Charles Lunalili, who ascended to the Hawaiian throne in 1873, was a monarch who advocated democracy and popular elections in his homeland.

The war boats of Otoo, king of Tahiti (at left), are put on display for Captain James Cook in April 1774, in a painting by William Hodges. European explorers first sailed to the Pacific in the 16th century in search of a western sea route to the Orient. Cook, an English seaman, explored many of the Pacific islands in the late 1700s. The "discovery" of the Pacific islands by Europeans and Americans greatly complicated the life of the islanders, as the newcomers' vision of the future of Oceania rarely coincided with the native population's wishes.

Cook spotted the Hawaiian islands on January 18, 1778. Although he was not their original discoverer, he called them the Sandwich Islands, a name that stuck for many years, in honor of his friend the earl of Sandwich. Initially, Cook and his crew were revered by the islanders (left), who believed that Cook was the reincarnation of their god Lono. Cook learned their language and was an honored guest and observer at many of their traditional ceremonies, such as human and animal sacrifices to a war god (above) and mock fights (below).

Cook and other explorers often brought artists with them to record the exotic scenery they discovered on their Pacific island voyages. Watercolorist John Webber depicted a variety of scenes from life in the Pacific islands, including this portrait of a man from the Sandwich Islands (at left) in 1780, an islander attending the burial site of his chief (above), and Europeans meeting natives of a New Zealand village (below).

The volcanic crater Kilauea on the island of Hawaii (above), as rendered by the American artist Titian Ramsay Peale. For many people the dramatic and unspoiled beauty of the Pacific islands represents paradise, and throughout history Pacific island settings have served as an inspiration for many artists.

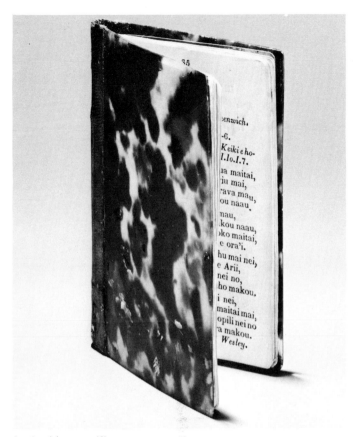

Christian missionaries in Hawaii created a phonetic alphabet that they used to translate their hymns and psalms into Hawaiian. In 1823 they created this hymnal on their own printing press and protected it between covers fashioned from turtle shell.

(continued from page 48)

Even the presence of a strong Hawaiian monarchy failed to stem the gradual deterioration of the islands. During the age of the monarchs, which lasted from 1795 to 1917, Hawaiians searched for a political identity that truly reflected their native culture, but the islands' rulers made no progress because they often worked at cross-purposes.

In 1872 more than a half-century of rule by the Kamehamehas ended with the death of King Kamehameha V. In 1873, King William Charles Lunalilo succeeded to the throne of Hawaii. During his year-long monarchy, William shepherded his homeland toward democracy by advocating popular elections and by supporting a constitution that limited the power of the king, but after his death in 1874, David Kalakaua

Christian missionary Dr. G. P. Judd stands between two future Hawaiian kings, Kamehameha IV and Kamehameha V, circa 1850, about 30 years after missionaries first came to the islands. Hawaii's royalty welcomed the missionaries' efforts to bring literacy to the general population.

assumed the kingship of Hawaii and worked hard to counter the reforms of his predecessor. King David wanted a return to a more traditional, autocratic form of government in which the king exercised the greatest authority in the land.

During King David's reign, which lasted from 1874 to 1891, the whaling and sandalwood industries collapsed, and the cultivation of sugar, usually on huge plantations, became a major economic force on the islands. The large plantations, owned predominantly by Americans, operated successfully only because Hawaii's monarchs sold scarce fertile land to the owners for a pittance. For example, Kamehameha V allowed plantation owners to buy the entire island of Niihau for very little money.

As the land holdings of the plantation owners grew, so too did their power. During the reign of King David Kalakaua they argued for and won a more favorable trade agreement that virtually eliminated all export taxes. Thereafter, the growers could ship their sugar to the mainland without losing more than a small percentage of their enormous profits to tariffs and duties. The plantation owners and sugar merchants also demanded greater say in the politics of the islands. They forced King David, virtually at gunpoint, to sign into law measures increasing the growers' political clout while limiting that of the Hawaiian people.

Control continued to slip from the monarchy during the brief reign of Queen Lydia Liliuokalani, who ascended the throne in 1891 after the death of her

Once foreigners began to come in large numbers to Hawaii, Hawaiians in turn grew more curious about the outside world. In 1881, King David Kalakaua (seated front, center) embarked on a 10-month journey around the world. His first stop was Japan, where he visited Prince Yoshiaki (front, left) and other dignitaries.

brother, King David Kalakaua. Queen Liliuokalani made a heroic effort to swing the balance of power back to the Hawaiian people. She also tried to impose a new constitution that would broaden the powers of the monarch, but these efforts aroused the ire of factions, led by the sugar and pineapple growers, determined to have Hawaii annexed by the United States. In 1894 these groups, backed by U.S. troops, abolished the monarchy and installed the wealthy and influential plantation owner Sanford Dole as governor of the islands.

U.S. president Benjamin Harrison had supported annexation and the abolition of the monarchy, but he was defeated in the 1892 presidential election by Grover Cleveland, who had other ideas. He was ap-

The last native monarch of Hawaii, Queen Lydia Liliuokalani, ruled from 1891 to 1893.

palled by the U.S. role in fomenting the coup that had overthrown Liliuokalani and agreed with his secretary of state's conclusion that the United States had exploited a "feeble but independent state." President Cleveland called for a restoration of the monarchy, but Dole and his supporters refused and proclaimed Hawaii a republic, with Dole as its president, on July 4, 1894. Because the revolution did not enjoy popular support, the republic's government continued to petition the United States for annexation and protection, but it was not until William McKinley succeeded Cleveland in 1897 that their pleadings were answered. Hawaii's autonomy officially came to an end on July 7, 1898, when McKinley signed into law a resolution that annexed the islands to the United States.

During the tumultuous period that followed the end of Queen Liliuokalani's reign, Hawaii briefly came under the rule of a provisional government composed of American businessmen from (left to right) James A. King, Sanford Dole, W. O. Smith, and P. C. Jones.

In the early 20th century, Main Street in Honolulu resembled the central thoroughfares of many towns on the mainland.

HAWAII: THE FIFTIETH STATE

As the 20th century began, the Hawaiians found themselves at a disadvantage in competing with the outsiders who were taking control of the islands. The Hawaiians' traditional generosity with money and material possessions was a liability in dealing with the acquisitive newcomers, who carefully guarded their financial holdings and increased their wealth throughout the years. Hawaiians also suffered because during the 19th century land ownership had come to be dominated by outsiders. Although in the late 1800s the Hawaiian government instituted land reform acts designed to restore land ownership to people of Hawaiian ancestry, virtually all the land suitable for farming and homesteading had already been sold, primarily to plantations and landholding companies. Despite the new laws, few Hawaiians were able to regain legal ownership of their native soil.

Hawaiians are able to claim at least one of the eight islands as solely their own. The small island of Niihau was purchased from Kamehameha V by an American family, the Robinsons, in 1864. The family vowed to preserve the island as a traditional Hawaiian community and closed it to all outsiders at the time of its purchase.

Niihau has changed little since that time. Most supplies still arrive by boat once a week. By design, the island lacks plumbing, electricity, and paved roads. As late as 1954 some news was still being brought to the island by carrier pigeon. The people of Niihau—where Hawaiian is the predominant language—center their lives around the church and pride themselves on their self-reliance. In 1982, when a hurricane swept through the island, its residents refused any help in rebuilding their community.

The world has not always allowed Niihau its privacy. When Japan launched a surprise attack on the U.S. military installations at Pearl Harbor on December 7, 1941, one of the Japanese planes crashed on Niihau. The islanders understood that something of great importance had happened when they saw the bullet-rid-

A member of the Robinson clan sits on horseback in front of one of the modest cottages the family provided for islanders on Niihau. The family bought the island in 1864 and then closed it to all outsiders in order to preserve Niihau's natural beauty.

dled plane, but they had no idea that the aircraft before them had helped spark a war. When the pilot admitted that his country had attacked Pearl Harbor, the islanders decided to send him via supply ship to the neighboring island of Kauai, where he could be taken into custody. But the ship did not arrive the next day as scheduled. After almost a week in captivity on Niihau, the pilot escaped and tried to hold the islands' residents hostage. He shot one of them, who became so enraged that he killed the pilot by throwing him against a wall.

Like Niihau, Kahoolawe is a Hawaiian island on which preservation and modernization are delicately balanced. Located off the coast of Maui, Kahoolawe is deserted and contains only ancient temples and shrines and military bombing targets. For over 40 years the island has provided the U.S. armed forces with their only mid-Pacific practice range. Kahoolawe's natural vegetation has been destroyed not only by shelling but also by the herds of wild goats that roam the barren landscape.

An organization called Protect Kahoolawe Ohanaò— *ohanaò* means "family" in Hawaiian—has tried to ban the target practice on an island they regard as sacred. For them this issue is symbolic of a past and present in which the Hawaiian people have been victimized by Western oppressors. The courts have sought to strike a balance between the needs of both sides in the issue and have ordered the ancient sites protected while still allowing bombing. Both sides have found it difficult to abide by the compromise.

A Melding of Peoples

The 20th century has brought a rapid and often unwanted transformation to Hawaii. Of all the changes, the loss of a truly Hawaiian population is perhaps the hardest for the Hawaiians themselves to endure. In addition to the large number of Americans and Europeans who came to the islands in the 1800s, a sizeable population of Chinese and, later, Japanese and Filipinos immigrated to Hawaii to work as contract laborers

After the great influx of whites to Hawaii, the islands became home to people of mixed ethnic background, including this young woman of Italian and Hawaiian ancestry.

on sugar and pineapple plantations. When their work obligations ended, Asian laborers frequently left the harsh life of the plantation to found their own businesses.

During the early 20th century, the Japanese became the single largest ethnic group in the islands, forming a tightly knit community that would later be an important base for political organization. By the time of World War II, the Japanese still constituted a clear majority. After the Japanese attack on Pearl Harbor, the United States declared martial law in the islands, fearing that Hawaii's Japanese would be loyal to Japan instead of the United States. By that time, only one-quarter of the islands' Japanese population had been born in Japan. The rest had been born in Hawaii.

On the U.S. mainland, a similar paranoia grew, and Americans of Japanese descent were put into internment camps, despite their being U.S. citizens. The Hawaiian islands became a command post and base of American operations for the Pacific, and Hawaiians of Japanese descent did what they could to demonstrate their loyalty and support. They were eager to fight for their country and eventually formed the 442nd Regimental Combat Team. The unit absorbed Hawaii's 100th Battalion, which was made up of Japanese Americans who had been inducted into the army before

The Chinese were the first Asians to migrate to Hawaii in great numbers. Most Chinese immigrants to Hawaii were men; the shortage of Chinese women led to many marriages between Chinese and Hawaiians.

This pineapple plantation on Oahu, photographed in the early 1900s, employed hundreds of workers from China and Japan. Asian immigrants on the plantations worked under brutal conditions and moved off as quickly as possible.

Pearl Harbor was attacked. These Japanese-American soldiers received great public acclaim for their valor in both the European and Pacific theaters of war.

A Renaissance of Culture

After World War II, the movement to establish statehood—begun soon after Hawaii became a territory—gained momentum. Virtually all segments of Hawaiian society favored statehood, and on August 21, 1959, Hawaii became the 50th member of the Union. Hawaii's new status brought with it an influx of tens of thousands of mainland Americans who dreamed of making their home in the beautiful setting of the South Pacific. These mid-20th-century arrivals encountered the same problem that Hawaiians had struggled with decades earlier: Most of the land was already owned.

Of all 50 states in the Union, only Connecticut, Delaware, and Rhode Island have a smaller land area than Hawaii, and much of Hawaii's land is covered by mountains or is otherwise impossible to develop. Close to half of the remaining land is owned by either the state or federal government. Private holding companies control a large percentage of what is left and rent it out to individuals. Together, the government and the largest holding companies account for 95 percent of the land in Hawaii. In order to break up these large holdings and return the land to individuals, the state government began condemning the land and selling it to prospective homeowners. This program has withstood many challenges in the courts and is likely to be more successful than the land reform acts of the previous century that sought to return the land directly to the Hawaiians.

The successful appropriation program of Hawaii's state government dramatizes an increased awareness of ancestral rights on the part of many Hawaiians. This growing sense of a shared land and history blossomed

The battleship USS Shaw explodes into flames after being attacked by Japanese bombers at Pearl Harbor. Although Hawaii had more Japanese residents than any state, relocation and internment took place only on the mainland.

during the late 1960s and early 1970s, when many Hawaiians promoted a renaissance of their traditional culture. One of the goals of this cultural rebirth was to instill a renewed sense of pride in their Polynesian ancestry among ethnic Hawaiians. The ancient Polynesians' feats as explorers and navigators became a subject of academic and popular interest. One team of anthropologists decided to re-create the ancient voyages of discovery undertaken by the seafaring Polynesians. The scientists built a full-sized voyaging canoe, loaded it with traditional crops and livestock, and dubbed it the *Hokule'a*, which is Hawaiian for "the star of gladness." (In English the star is known as Arcturus.)

The headline of the Honolulu Star-Bulletin *tells the story: On August 21, 1959, Hawaii became the 50th state in the Union.*

The aim of the project was to complete a round trip between Hawaii and Tahiti, navigating only by traditional methods. A Micronesian, Pius Mau Piailug, acted as the navigator, and Hawaiians made up most of the crew. Celebration and traditional ceremonies and rituals accompanied the ship's departure. The journey from Hawaii to Tahiti, across 3,700 miles of open ocean, was completed in 35 days. The return voyage, using a Tahitian navigator, was accomplished in 22 days. (The shorter time resulted from better weather.)

Traditional values rekindled during the 1970s live on in Hawaii. There are luaus at times of celebration, such as marriages, which strengthen bonds between individuals and the community. Along with such traditional fare as fresh seafood and roast pork, Hawaiians serve such new refreshments as beer. Hawaiian celebrations form the chief social events of large fam-

The ethnic reawakening of the late 1960s and early 1970s manifested itself in Hawaii in a renewed interest in the culture and achievements of the ancient Polynesians. The construction and voyage of the Ohokuleao, *an accurate facsimile of a Polynesian vessel, was merely one example of this revival.*

These hula dancers were just a few of the 41,000 native Hawaiians who assembled in Honolulu's Aloha Stadium to commemorate Hawaiian Unity Day in 1988. Hawaiian islanders make great efforts to keep traditions such as the hula and the luau alive in modern Hawaii.

ilies, which continue to be the norm. A long-standing joke in the islands pokes fun at this tendency: "I'm going to have a small family. I'm only going to have nine kids." Families continue to adopt children, either formally or informally, even when they already have many. A Hawaiian quoted by author Francine Grey in her book *Hawaii: The Sugar Coated Fortress* provides an example of the Hawaiians' generous attitude toward kinship:

> This girl, my daughter, is my brother's child [says a woman speaking about her adopted daughter]. Of course, my brother isn't really my brother, as he and I are adopted children of my father. I guess my father isn't really my father, is he? I know who my real mother is, but I don't like her and I never see her. My adopted brother is half Hawaiian and I am pure Hawaiian. We aren't

really any blood relation, I guess, but I always think of him as my brother. I think maybe my adopted father is really my grandfather's brother. I am not sure, as we never asked such things.

A Living Tradition

Old traditions such as large families and group celebrations have outlasted many other changes that have swept over the Hawaiian islands. On holidays or at special events visitors can experience the mystical beauty and driving rhythms of Hawaiian folk chants, orations, and the hula, an ancient Hawaiian dance form in which each movement stands for a specific word. Hula dancers create stories and prayers through a series of intricate gestures and steps. The contemporary practice of the hula is just one way that Hawaiians have managed to hold on to the strongest elements of their tradition in the face of overwhelming change.

POLYNESIANS: CHALLENGES OF THEIR OWN

Hawaii's eight islands constitute only a small portion of Polynesia. Throughout this island landscape, many other groups of people have, like the Hawaiians, faced cultural extinction caused by contact with the West. In general, Polynesians shared a cultural heritage similar to that of the Hawaiians, but each island group—isolated from the rest—developed its own distinct set of rituals and practices.

As it became evident to the Hawaiians that their loss of land and declining population would leave them with little say in the governance of their own islands, some argued that they should have met the outsiders with violence rather than friendship, as the Maori, the aboriginal inhabitants of New Zealand, had done. But resistance had done the Maori little good. Although New Zealand is 16 times larger than Hawaii, the Maori retained less than 6 percent of their land. Only an extremely small portion was suitable for farming; most of it was located in remote and less desirable areas.

Located in the southernmost corner of the Polynesian triangle, New Zealand was explored by Captain Cook in 1769. Approximately 200,000 Maori lived there during Cook's four visits, which took place between 1769 and 1777. Upon his return home he described his "discovery" in vivid detail, thus attracting a hoard of whalers, traders, and missionaries to this corner of Polynesia. By 1840 the first permanent English settlement, Wellington, had been founded in New Zealand.

At first, the Maori tended to get along better with the white settlers than with each other. As in Hawaii, the introduction of European guns, which the Maori used in intertribal wars, drastically reduced the native population. Missionaries, anxious to provide what they saw as the benefits of English society, tried to end the violence among the Maori by preaching the Christian gospel to them. The Maori treated them with great respect overall, but the clergy's efforts could not prevent the confrontation that was about to erupt.

In 1860 war broke out between the Maori and the English over the settlers' insatiable desire for Maori land. The *pakeha* (white men) seized huge parcels of acreage despite Maori attempts to stop them. The conflict lasted through 12 years of intermittent fighting.

In a photograph from about 1910, New Zealand Maoris stand outside a typical Polynesian straw-roofed dwelling.

The disharmony that had prevailed among the different Maori tribes even prior to the arrival of the pakeha helped contribute to their defeat. The tribes took different sides—some sided with the pakeha and some fought against them. Their opponents' lack of unity hastened the whites' victory. Much of the Maori's land was confiscated and awarded to white settlers.

After the war the Maori tried to revive their community by living as a separate society. Some returned to farming and succeeded in cultivating an abundant crop more frequently than did white settlers. In the early 1900s the Maori land was absorbed into the domain of British New Zealand. The government gave the native islanders some official representation and sought to protect the Maori people against the ill effects of civilization. As the 20th century progressed, it gradually became evident that many of the laws which were meant to aid the Maori—such as laws regulating the sale of alcohol—actually discriminated against them. These laws were gradually eliminated.

As the 20th century nears its end, the Maori face the difficult task of maintaining traditional values in a contemporary society that seems to place little value upon them. The Maori population is once again expanding, but with an unfortunate side effect: Their land is being divided into smaller and smaller plots with the passing of each generation. One of the most difficult questions the Maori face today is how to pass the limited remaining land from parents to their descendants without running out of territory.

Monuments of a Lost Culture

Contact with the West certainly undermined the traditional societies of both the Hawaiians and the Maori. But Westerners are not to blame for the deterioration of all Polynesian societies. The 1,300-year-old community of Easter Island was already in a state of collapse when it first encountered Europeans. On Easter Sunday, 1722, Dutch explorers first sighted the land they later called Easter Island, which is located at the easternmost point of the Polynesian triangle.

These carved monoliths, known as moais, *are smaller versions of the giant sculptures for which Easter Island—located more than 2,000 miles off the coast of Chile—is known.*

The Polynesians on Easter Island had developed a sophisticated and complex culture. In honor of their chiefs, they carved huge statues out of the hillsides. These stone totems averaged 20 feet in height and weighed up to 90 tons. The Easter Islanders used sleds and ropes to move their massive sculptures to holy places. But by the 18th century, artistic achievement had lost its importance among the islanders, who struggled just to survive.

The European explorers found the remaining inhabitants of the once-great society living in caves. They had been driven from their homes by a continual state of war on the island. Overcrowding had also helped devastate Easter Island's natural resources. Isolated and small, measuring only 64 square miles, the island could not support the demands of its rapidly expanding population, which numbered more than 7,000 at its peak. The surviving inhabitants were in no shape to resist the encroachment of European civilization. By the 1860s virtually the entire population of Easter Island had been forcibly rounded up and shipped to South America aboard slave boats.

In 1888 the South American country of Chile annexed Easter Island for the same reason that the United States had claimed Hawaii as a territory: the island's strategic location in the Pacific. Today, Easter Island is used as a refueling and rest stop for Chilean airliners en route to Australia. Its visitors include archaeologists who study the colossal monuments for which Easter Island has become famous. More than perhaps any other place in Oceania, Easter Island remains a testament to the greatness that was lost with the destruction of so much of Oceania's culture.

Landscape painter William Hodges accompanied Cook on his second voyage and rendered this eerie portrayal of Easter Island when the expedition landed there in March 1774. The skull and bones in the right foreground are intended to symbolize the extinct civilization of the monoliths' creators.

The Two Samoas

The term Samoa refers not to a single island, but to two halves of an island chain: Western Samoa and American Samoa, the only United States territory lying south of the equator. Western Samoa contains the islands Savaii and Upolu and seven satellite islands. American Samoa is composed of the eastern part of the chain and includes Tutuila, the Manua Islands, and Swains Island. First settled by Polynesians in approximately 1000 B.C., Samoa came to the attention of Europeans in 1722, when it was sighted by the Dutch explorer Jacob Roggeveen. During the next century,

An impoverished section of Pago Pago. The house at rear has retained the customary shape of traditional Polynesian dwellings, but in a humble concession to modernity, tin has replaced thatch as the building's roof.

A teacher in Pago Pago instructs young students—dressed in both traditional and Western garments—in the grammar of their native tongue.

Britain, Germany, and the United States vied for control of Samoa. In order to appease these world powers, Samoan chiefs granted trading privileges to the United States in 1878 and to Britain and Germany the following year.

In 1899 the United States formalized its relationship with Samoa by annexing Eastern Samoa—all but Swains Island—in a treaty signed between the U.S. and Samoan governments. (Swains Island became part of American Samoa when it was annexed in 1925.) American Samoa was administered by the U.S. Navy until 1951, when that responsibility passed to the Department of the Interior. Western Samoa, meanwhile, was claimed by Germany, which retained its control until World War I. In 1918, New Zealand wrested the islands from German hands; Samoans lived under the rule of New Zealand for the next 44 years, until 1962, when the islanders won their independence and declared their homeland the Independent State of Western Samoa.

In American Samoa the traditional communal society has been incorporated into the modern political structure. The time-honored class structure of a ruling caste and commoners has been preserved, but democratic elements have been introduced. Clan chiefs, known as *matai*, are still responsible for watching over their people, but the matai are now elected to their post. Most are the kin of previous matai, however. In each individual village the *matolo* is the highest authority. He parcels out communally owned farmland, oversees village finances, and makes sure that the community runs smoothly.

The two Samoas share a common culture. Although American Samoa enjoys more economic advantages than its counterpart to the west, both are highly dependent on foreign aid—Western Samoa on New Zealand and American Samoa on the United States. It is quite easy for American Samoans to join the U.S. military or become American citizens, and many have made use of these opportunities to leave the islands. There are twice as many Samoans living on the West Coast of the United States as there are in American Samoa, and a sizable Samoan community also resides in Hawaii.

The Ancient Kingdom of Tonga

The kingdom of Tonga is another island group that has clung to its traditional mode of life. Located to the southwest of American Samoa, Tonga comprises approximately 170 islands, which fall into three groups: Tongatapu, Haapai, and Vavau. Tonga is the last surviving monarchy of the Pacific. From 1900 to 1968 Tonga was a British protectorate, but it always governed itself. In 1968 the British and the Tongans signed a new treaty, which substantially reduced British control in the region. Just two years later, Tonga won its independence and declared itself a constitutional monarchy.

Three thousand years ago, Tonga, along with Samoa, acted as a base for voyaging islanders exploring the farthest reaches of the Pacific. Tongans still value their distinguished heritage, including their ancient lineage of kings, which dates back almost 1,000 years. Since 1845 Tonga has been ruled by the Tupou dynasty. Although the political system is predominantly controlled by men, women have occupied key positions in the aristocracy and some have reigned. Queen Salote Tupou III ruled from 1918 to 1965. In addition, female members of the Tupou family have the honor of serving as ceremonial leaders at family functions.

Although politically stable, Tongan society has undergone great change. In the 20th century, the extended family—central to the life of most Tongans—has suffered as people leave their villages in search of better jobs, both in the capital city of Nukualofa (located on Tongatapu) and in Hawaii and California. Most Tongans learn English as a second language in their schools and therefore have an advantage over other immigrant groups in building a new life in America.

Three Tongans, all wearing skirts woven from rushes, hold a grass mat and a fish—two items they presented to a Dutch expedition led by Abel Tasman that visited Tonga in 1643. Tasman was amazed by the "peace and amity" of the islands; Cook, who landed there 143 years later, was so taken by the amiability of the natives that he dubbed the region the Friendly Islands.

A photograph from the U.S. Army Stragetic Defense Command shows the trails of missles launched from California as they approach their targets on Kwajalein Atoll in the Marshall Islands.

MICRONESIA

Approximately 420 years ago Spain claimed title to the more than 2,100 islands of Micronesia, which are grouped in three archipelagoes known today as the Marshall, Caroline, and Mariana islands. The Spanish used the islands as a supply station for voyages between Mexico and the Philippines, which were then just two of its many colonies. Spain retained control of the islands until the end of the 19th century, when defeat in the Spanish-American War in 1898 forced the former world power to yield its Pacific holdings, including Micronesia. Spain surrendered the island of Guam, located in the Mariana archipelago, to the United States and sold the rest of the islands to Germany for a mere $4 million.

In the 20th century, Micronesia has changed hands twice as a result of war. After World War I, Germany lost the islands to Japan, which in turn relinquished them at the end of World War II to a newly formed international peacekeeping organization, the United Nations (UN). The UN decided to place the islands under the trusteeship of the United States. Americans had become familiar with Micronesia during the war, when the islands had proven to be invaluable to the U.S. military as a jumping-off point for attacks on the Japanese.

In February 1945 the U.S. Navy and Marine Corps launched a historic attack on the Japanese island strongholds of Iwo Jima and Okinawa from the Mari-

Ferocious fighting between Japanese and American forces destroyed many parts of Guam during World War II, as attested to by this photograph taken in 1944.

anas, and in August 1945, American military aircraft flew from the island of Tinian to the Japanese cities of Hiroshima and Nagasaki, where they ushered in the nuclear age by dropping two atomic bombs. The islands of Micronesia are still littered with the remains of World War II as well as with the remnants of stone monuments from a more ancient past, when Micronesia belonged to Micronesians alone. Anxious to have their autonomy restored, some of the islands are now negotiating with the United States in order to achieve their independence.

In the early 1980s the Republic of the Marshall Islands agreed to a Compact of Free Association with the U.S. government, which went into effect October 21, 1986. This agreement allows the Micronesian people to govern themselves internally yet still receive U.S. military protection and the guidance of American foreign policy makers. Under the terms of the treaty, the United States also continues to provide financial support and assures the people of the Micronesian republics the right to travel and to obtain U.S. residency. In fact, since 1950, inhabitants of the island of Guam have been eligible not only for residency in the United States but also for citizenship.

American monetary aid helps fund health care, education, and municipal improvements, such as the building of airport runways. (In spite of these measures, many residents must journey to Guam or Hawaii to receive advanced medical treatment or higher education.) Most islands depend on American dollars because the governments of these small republics have few ways to generate income. The vast majority of Micronesia's islands have only the sea and a limited amount of fertile land as natural resources. One lucky exception to this rule is the island of Nauru, which contains rich phosphate deposits it can sell to mining companies. Although some of this profit buys goods and services for the islanders, most of it is invested for the day when the mineral resources run dry.

Janet McCoy served as the last administrator of the U.S. trust territory before the Marshall Islands obtained their autonomy.

The Nuclear Pacific

Although their relationship with the United States does benefit Pacific Islanders in many ways, it also presents many drawbacks. In the years following World War II, the U.S. military incorporated Micronesia into its Pacific strategy, resulting in a sizable American military presence on the islands. In the Republic of the Marshall Islands, for example, the Kwajalein atoll is home to an American missile base. The United States pays the island government millions of dollars each year for the use of the land and also hires some workers from surrounding islands. Islanders feel that the United States's reliance on their homeland for military and strategic reasons makes it less inclined to give them a greater say in governing themselves. They also worry that the presence of U.S. military installations makes the islands a possible target of foreign attack.

Even more controversial than the missile base and the U.S. military presence are the events that took place in another area of the Marshall Islands. In the first 20 years after World War II, Bikini and the less well known Eniwetok—two atolls in the Marshall group—were the site of 66 nuclear explosions, including that of the first hydrogen bomb. Radioactive fallout caused by the bombs polluted the region, making it uninhabitable.

The story of Bikini's people in the nuclear age illustrates the fragility of traditional societies in the 20th century. When Bikini residents were evacuated by the U.S. government before the first nuclear test, they were assured that they would be able to return to their island in a few years. At that time little was known about the long-term contamination caused by nuclear weapons. The atolls to which they were moved proved disastrous for the islanders, according to Robert Trumbull, author of *Tin Roofs and Palm Trees: A Report on the New South Seas.*

> The reluctant migration of the 167 unhappy Bikinians took them first to Rongerik, then to Kwajalein, and finally to Kili island, a lonely outcropping at the southern end of the Ralik

chain [of the Marshall Islands]. . . .The island was rainier than Bikini and significantly smaller, without the fish resources of a lagoon. To cultivate the strange soil, the Bikinians had to learn how to grow food plants that had not existed in their previous environment. Violent seas completely isolated the island for many months in the year. . . . [Islanders] told me that the forlorn little community—swollen to more than 300 by then—had been hungry on occasion for weeks at a time.

The U.S. government paid Bikinians $3 million to compensate them for the loss of their home island, but no monetary amount could purchase the return of the island as it once had been or restore its traditional culture. Today, the children of displaced Bikini islanders are no longer taught to farm and fish in coastal waters, as their parents and grandparents did before them. As members of the older generation die, these skills are lost to their descendants forever.

The U.S. Navy relocated natives of the atoll of Bikini to Rongerik so that the island could be used to test atomic weapons. Here navy personnel erect cisterns that will catch rainwater for drinking. The facilities provided by the U.S. government proved grossly inadequate for the Micronesians, many of whom still live in poverty as a result of being banished from their homeland.

Change and Stability

Throughout Micronesia, the traditional occupations of farming and fishing can no longer sustain the region's population. Each year, thousands leave the outer islands and move to larger towns and cities in the South Pacific. A new, urban generation that has never known the sea and land has grown to adulthood. Many do not want to return from their new homes in the cities to the difficult life of the outer islands, an existence that offers few material rewards and requires tremendous physical stamina. On some of the more isolated isles, for example, obtaining food and supplies can still require journeys by boat or canoe of up to 100 miles.

In addition, many Pacific Islanders born after World War II lack the specialized skills needed to survive outside urban centers. They no longer possess the ability to make crops grow in poor soil or to build the lightweight boats needed to sail quickly from one small island to the next. However, islanders have welcomed the loss of some traditional ways. The ancient class system, which discriminated against both women and the members of the lower castes, virtually disappeared during the 1950s and 1960s. Today, children from varied family backgrounds frequently attend the same schools, and the Micronesian work force is no longer segregated based on class rather than ability. Unlike their forebears, Micronesians of the late 20th century have become politically sophisticated and can meet foreign powers as equals in the field of diplomacy. Those in government try to reap the advantages of modernity while also preserving what they can of their native culture. In some islands' constitutions, for example, the special status of the chiefs, traditionally the leaders of the community, is guaranteed by law instead of by custom alone.

The already difficult task of governing a territory spread out over thousands of miles of ocean is complicated by the many cultural differences among the Micronesians. The people in one island group often object to being represented by someone from another group. Differences often date back thousands of years to ancient times and are especially pronounced be-

Guamanian leader Ron Rivera heads the Organization of People for Indigenous Rights (OPIR), a group fighting to restore self-determination to the people of Guam.

tween residents of large islands and those from small atolls.

People on the atolls led much more tenuous lives because they had to travel great distances to get what they needed. As a result of their travels, they were often more worldly than were the people of the large islands. But because the atolls could not support a population large enough to form an army, the larger islands had the advantage of military strength and controlled their smaller neighbors, forcing them to pay tribute for protection. Today the people of these atolls still regard those from large islands as potential oppressors and dread falling under their rule.

In May 1988, Ben Blaz (center), congressman from Guam, posed with Guamanian women in native dress during Asian-American heritage week at the Dover Air Force Base in Delaware.

PACIFIC ISLANDERS IN THE UNITED STATES

The vast majority of Pacific Islander immigrants to the United States are native inhabitants of one of four islands: American Samoa and Tonga, both located in Polynesia; and Guam and Saipan, two islands in the Mariana chain of Micronesia. Once in the United States, they form communities—virtual islands within the broader cultural mix of America—that provide the economic, social, and emotional support necessary to a successful transition from island to mainland. Existing primarily in and around major West Coast cities, such as Los Angeles and San Francisco, each of these communities reflects the unique character of its Pacific origin.

Pacific Islanders first traveled to the United States as members of the crews of American trading ships and whalers more than a century ago, but they did not arrive in significant numbers until the 1950s. During that decade the U.S. government offered resident status to inhabitants of its Pacific trust territories. Legislation regarding Guam broadened the proposal to include citizenship as well as residency.

Late 20th-century Pacific Islanders migrate to the United States for much the same reason that they flock to larger towns and urban centers in their homeland—

better economic opportunity. One factor that has spurred emigration to the United States is the dramatic increase in the islands' population. Between 1980 and 1985, for example, the population of Guam increased 16.8 percent, that of the Mariana Islands jumped 14 percent, and the population of American Samoa grew by 12.4 percent. The growth of employment has lagged far behind that of population, forcing thousands of Pacific Islanders to leave home each year in search of jobs. Additional incentives for emigration include a high rate of inflation and the loss of farming—the traditional means of survival—as a viable way of sustaining a characteristically large Pacific Islander family.

Guamanians and Other Micronesians

Many residents of the U.S. trust territories find jobs as civilian employees on American military bases in the Pacific. Because they are U.S. citizens, Guamanians have the additional option of joining the armed forces. Many have entered the navy as a means of paying for their transit to the United States and of guaranteeing financial security once they have arrived. Guamanian civilians have found that the American military is their greatest single employer after they migrate to the United States. According to Bradd Shorr, an expert on the Pacific Islander community in the United States, most immigrants from Guam live near large naval shipyards located on America's West Coast. About 20,000 Guamanians—virtually all of them Chamorros, people of mixed Filipino, Spanish, and Guamanian stock who constitute the great majority of all Guamanians—reside in San Diego; 10,000 live in Los Angeles; another 10,000 have made their home in San Francisco, and 2,000 to 3,000 now live in the Seattle-Tacoma area of Washington State.

Guamanians and other immigrants from Micronesia find the educational opportunities in the United States as attractive as the chance to advance economically. The story of John Uruo, a resident of Puluwat—located in the Caroline Islands—in many ways typifies that of Pacific Islanders from this region. In 1968, at age 21, Uruo gathered with a group of his extended family and friends at a farewell feast held in his honor.

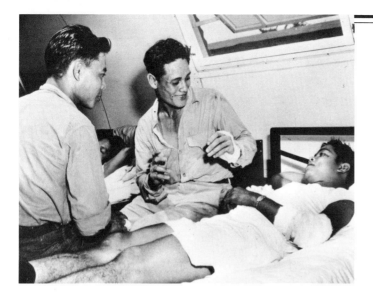

American and Guamanian soldiers recover from wounds in a military hospital during World War II. Many Guamanian men enter the U.S. military, which is the single largest employer on the island.

According to the October 1986 edition of *National Geographic* magazine:

> John at his leave-taking drew a large crowd who brought to the feast homegrown bounty—roast pig, fried fish, boiled breadfruit, taro root and leaf cooked in coconut milk, small sweet bananas, and coconut wine.
>
> After the elders' speeches John rose. "I go to jump over the wall," he said.
>
> The wall John went to leap was figurative, built of conditions that separated him and fellow islanders from today's world—isolation, poor health and education, and few financial resources. In good health, John had a plan to overcome the others. He would go to college in the United States—the first from his island to do so.

John Uruo attended Bemidji State University in Minnesota on scholarship. He adjusted to American culture as successfully as he acclimated himself to the subzero temperatures of midwestern winters. After graduating, Uruo chose to marry an American woman and had two daughters with her, but he felt torn between the homeland he loved and his adopted country. Like many Micronesians he maintained strong ties to relatives in the Pacific, and ultimately he decided that he had a duty to serve his community. Yet Uruo knew that Puluwat lacked the excellent public schools so common in the United States. He struck a compromise, deciding to return to Puluwat himself, but allowing his daughters to remain with their mother in America in order to reap the benefits of the educational system on the mainland.

Like John Uruo, Pacific Islanders are particularly hard hit by conflicts between their many family and community obligations, which tie them closely to their island of origin, and the desire to enjoy greater material, educational, and vocational advantages available only in the United States. Each island's particular history and culture helps to determine how its people will overcome the difficulties common to most Pacific communities trying to establish themselves in a new country.

The Strength of the Samoan Community

Although residents of American Samoa do not enjoy U.S. citizenship—as Guamanians do—they can migrate to America as U.S. nationals. This status confers on them the right of free entry into the country. The relative ease of immigration has brought tens of thousands of Samoans—estimates range from 40,000 to 60,000—into the United States. Of this number approximately 15 to 20 percent arrive from Western rather than American Samoa. Nearly 20,000 Samoans live in or around Los Angeles, most in the neighboring

In 1972, Samoan high chief Nofoaluma Tuiasosopo founded Samoa Mo Samoa, a San Francisco organization that promotes self-determination for American Samoa.

communities of Carson, Long Beach, Oceanside, and Wilmington. About 10,000 to 15,000 Samoans reside in the San Francisco area. Nearly 6,000 call San Diego home, and another 2,000 live in Seattle. Pockets of Samoans—chiefly those who belong to the Mormon church—have established communities in Salt Lake City, Utah, and St. Louis, Missouri. Many Samoans have also migrated to Hawaii, where approximately 10,000 of them now live.

No new arrival from Samoa is likely to feel isolated, because more Samoans live in the United States than in American Samoa. Samoan communities, while maintaining a strong bond to their islands, have adapted their native culture to that of the United States. For example, the title of chief, or matai, has been reduced in importance in America because the authority and responsibility the office carries has little relevance to life in the United States.

In fact, the traditional social system of Samoa is quickly fading within Samoan-American communities throughout the United States. An increasing number of Samoan Americans are born in North America, and these younger people balk at many of the customs of Samoan society, which they view as restrictive. Younger Samoan Americans respect age and position but for the most part have declined to preserve the formal title of matai within their communities. Now finances and important decisions are left to the adults who head families.

These differences among generations have perhaps been accelerated because over the years the background of the people coming to the mainland has changed. In the early 1950s, most of the Samoans who immigrated to the United States were in the military and usually came from the islands' larger cities. More recently, Samoan immigrants have come from rural areas, in search of better economic and educational opportunities. The newer arrivals tend to be much less concerned than their wealthier predecessors with maintaining the traditional class system of Samoa.

Another aspect of Samoan life that has changed in America is the physical composition of the community. People no longer have to live next door to each other

On the American mainland, many Samoan women—such as this cafeteria employee—work in service industries on army bases and in hospitals.

to feel that they are neighbors and friends because they can easily journey across town by car or speak on the telephone. These modern conveniences have helped preserve the extended family, an institution crucial to the majority of Samoans, especially those new to the United States.

Immigrant families who have recently arrived in the United States from the Pacific islands usually make their home with relatives of either the husband or the wife. Such stays not infrequently stretch into months and even years. Usually, several interrelated families live within several miles of each other, so that visiting relatives can move from household to household and reduce the burden of financial and emotional support placed on any one family.

When a relative comes to stay, he or she automatically becomes part of the daily life of the household, contributing money for grocery and utility bills and participating in necessary chores such as cleaning, baby-sitting, and yard work. Relatives who come from the islands provide a very important helping hand, especially, as is often the case, when both parents work. This help is so valuable that many families on the mainland send money back to the islands to help bring relatives over. In *New Neighbors . . . Islanders in Adaptation*, a collection of accounts of immigrants from the Pacific Islands, a young Samoan newcomer describes how his responsibilities to his family and friends did not lessen upon immigrating:

> The Samoan is born into a regulated, regimented society. If you are living with relatives in the United States, you are still required to contribute your part to the family. You are expected to do all your household tasks before you do your homework, no matter how much homework you have. If you are living with friends here, you have the same problem.

The network of family relations forms a base for the community, and the community at large often works as an extension of the family by helping its members find jobs or by providing for their needs in times of crisis. Each family has occasions when it must turn to others for aid, but those who depend on the community must also lend a hand when misfortune befalls Samoan friends and neighbors. Each family undergoes the scrutiny of the others. For example, families that lend significant amounts of money to others receive generous loans when they are in difficulty, while families that make only small contributions receive little in return. If a person or family is always in need—and thus unable to provide any support for the community—other Samoans will collectively buy them a ticket back home.

A Samoan skier takes to the slopes in Jackson Hole, Wyoming. Samoan Americans have adapted easily to American customs and culture.

A Samoan-American Family

In many ways the Levis—who were interviewed by reporters for the *San Francisco Chronicle* in 1989—epitomize the Samoan-American family. For 20 years the Levis have made their home in the San Bruno district of San Francisco. Their 2-bedroom house has provided shelter for as many as 11 people at a time, including Fanuaea Levi, the matriarch of the clan; her 3 daughters, and an assortment of sons-in-law, children, grandchildren, and great-grandchildren. In the mid-1960s, Fanuaea Levi bought the San Bruno house with an inheritance from her husband, a naval petty officer.

The vast majority of Samoan Americans have settled in either Hawaii or in West Coast cities such as San Francisco, home to this grocer of Samoan descent.

In 1989 she still received government retirement benefits from the navy, her main source of income.

One of Levi's married daughters, Lina Tufono, told the *Chronicle*: "This home is the center of the family. People are always stopping by to say hi, to get something to eat, to check in on mom." Like many Samoan Americans of her generation, Lina Tufono is a devoted child. She cooks for her mother, chauffeurs her to the Samoan Congregational Church of Jesus Christ, and includes her in all family activities.

All of Fanuaea Levi's three daughters and their spouses split household expenses, but they have expressed resentment at the large financial burden placed on them by the surrounding Samoan-American community. The Levis, like all Samoans, have donated up to $500 to other families at times of celebration or hardship. In the words of one of the daughters, "It's been a bad year. We've had seven weddings and funerals."

Despite their adherence to this Samoan tradition, the Levi family faces a rapid acculturation into the American mainstream and, with that assimilation, the loss of Samoan identity. According to the *Chronicle*:

> Living with generations together has allowed even the grandchildren to speak a bit of Samoan. But they do it infrequently, usually when speaking to their grandmother, who doesn't speak much English. Living together has kept Samoan food on the family dinner table. But, slowly, that tradition has given way. Nowadays, the family's meal of choice more often is spaghetti, Chinese food, or burgers and fries from McDonald's.

Like all immigrant families, the Levis and other Pacific Islander families face the challenge of preserving their unique heritage while also participating in the main-stream of American society.

The Church and the Samoan Community

Fanuaea Levi's active participation in her church mirrors the devotion of many Samoan Americans to their local place of worship. The church plays a central role in the West Coast Samoan community, just as it does in the islands. It provides a place for the community to gather and so serves both spiritual and social needs. Besides religious services, most Samoan-American churches offer social events that are organized by the congregants. Taken together, these events offer participants a full and active community life. In fact, in America, the church has replaced the village as the source of the Samoans' community identity. Membership in a church bonds thousands of families and individuals in a common appreciation of Samoan heritage.

The history of Samoa itself is reflected in the churches Samoans choose today. In the early days of Samoa's contact with the West, the London Missionary Society acted as the center of Christianity on the island. Today in Samoa, the Protestant Congregational churches that have developed from the work of the London Missionary Society have the largest membership. Churches whose representatives arrived in the islands later have smaller congregations. Church membership in the United States follows a similar pattern. The most popular churches are Congregational churches either similar to or connected with those back home. Other churches—such as Methodist, Roman Catholic, and Mormon—have fewer congregants on the mainland, just as they do on the islands.

The major difference in church attendance on the mainland is in the frequency with which Samoans move between churches, either of the same or a different denomination. As a result of this movement, Samoans on the mainland have a greater say in their own religious life than they had on the islands. A number of families can decide to form their own church, choosing one of their group to serve as minister. The ministers of the churches on the West Coast are different from their island counterparts, however, in that they usually receive little financial support from the community. In the islands, the minister's status resembles that of a matai, and he receives generous compensation from the community.

In the United States, Samoans have found a greater variety of churches available to them and have sometimes decided to move to a church—such as a fundamentalist Pentecostal denomination—that does not have a strong foothold in the islands. In the course of adapting to life in America, Samoans have adhered to a strong religious tradition while at the same time taking advantage of the new possibilities presented by life in the larger West Coast communities.

Tonga's Challenge

Unlike Guamanians and Samoans, Tongans have had great difficulty in adjusting to the culture and customs of America. Their trouble is rooted in the extremely formalized class structure in which many Tongans were—and still are—raised. For example, one Tongan immigrant, described in *New Neighbors . . . Islanders in Adaption*, found that his manner with superiors worked against him in the United States, although at home his behavior would have been regarded as correct and polite.

At 9:00 A.M. Situveni came to the factory and went into the interviewer's office without knocking. He sat down without having been invited to do so, as is the Tongan custom. Initially, he had nothing to say, because it was not his right to speak first in someone else's *fale* [home]. When he was addressed by the American employer, Situveni, following Tongan custom, showed respect according to his formal childhood training, by not looking directly at the man's eyes. He kept his head down and looked away. His answers were abrupt.

The interviewer found the Tongan's behavior strange, and because he would not make eye contact, thought the prospective employee was trying to hide something. Situveni failed to get the job.

Although they face greater obstacles to their successful adjustment to life in the United States, Tongan Americans share many similarities with other Pacific Islanders. As with fellow Polynesians and Micronesians, they benefit from a tightly knit community, which provides them with financial and emotional support when needed. Births, weddings, and deaths serve as occasions that bring the family together.

A young Tongan-American volunteers an answer in her classroom in Oakland, California. California and Hawaii are home to the majority of Tongans in the United States.

Unfortunately, the strong sense of ethnic identity common to Pacific Islanders has not helped distinguish them in the eyes of most other Americans. People from the Pacific often find themselves confused with people of other nationalities. For example, until recently many official forms lacked a category for people of Pacific origin. One American of Pacific Island extraction relates the following experience which took place in the late 1970s:

I am an advisor for the Los Angeles City Schools. The school superintendent called me and said, "Lei, I remember you once said your grandfather was Chinese. The Asian Commission has called

Volunteer workers at Samoa Mo Samoa are just a few of the Pacific Islanders who are organizing to demand recognition of their unique ethnic background.

us wanting to know how many Asians we have on our staff. May I count you as an Asian?" I said, "No, I am a Polynesian." And he said, "Then you're an Asian." . . . I told the superintendent, "No, I am not an Asian. I am Polynesian." And he said, "Well, there's no category for that."

Experiences like these have angered Pacific Islanders and mobilized them into organizing such groups as the Pacific/Asian Coalition, established in 1972. In Hawaii, men and women descended from the original inhabitants of the islands have formed Hawaiians United, Inc. As a result of the latter organization's work, the category *Hawaiian* finally appeared on the 1980 census. This victory is of more than symbolic importance to Hawaiians because government and private agencies use census information to decide how to allocate funds in certain communities. Hawaiians found that without proof of their numbers they were easily denied federal grants for which they should have been eligible.

In fact, Hawaii has led all states in its recognition of many Pacific Island groups because each island group has a larger community in Hawaii than in any other state. In the 50th state, Micronesians and Polynesians coexist with whites and Asian Americans in a balance found nowhere else in the world.

Indeed, the Hawaiian islands have been described as a model multiracial society. That does not mean that the diverse communities there always get along, but given the ethnic and religious diversity found there, a remarkable harmony exists. But that harmony rests upon the continued efforts of Hawaii's residents to work together.

Both on Hawaii and the mainland, Pacific Islanders founded communities based on the traditions they knew. Because a shared ancestry and similar cutural heritage unites all islanders, their communities share many common traits and many dilemmas. In some ways, their problems are the difficulties faced by all immigrants—the need for housing, employment, and acceptance by other Americans. The vast majority of Pacific Islanders have realized many of their goals in coming to the United States. Their strong community ties and willingness to aid one another have proven invaluable to this effort. But even with these advantages, Pacific Islanders have continually faced the problem of balancing a new culture with the carefully preserved remnants of the old. As has been true of other immigrant groups before them, the degree to which Pacific Islanders resolve this issue will help determine their success in the United States.

FURTHER READING

Bellwood, Peter. *The Polynesians: Prehistory of an Island People.* London: Thames & Hudson, 1978.

Brower, Kenneth. *Micronesia: The Land, the People and the Sea.* Baton Rouge: Louisiana State University Press, 1981.

Bunge, Fredrica M., ed. *Oceania: A Regional Study.* Washington, DC: U.S. Government Printing Office, 1984.

Grattan, C. Hartley. *The Southwest Pacific to 1900.* Ann Arbor: University of Michigan Press, 1963.

Howard, Alan. *Ain't No Big Thing: Coping Strategies in a Hawaiian-American Community.* Honolulu: University of Hawaii Press, 1974.

Jennings, Jesse D. *The Prehistory of Polynesia.* Canberra: Australian National University Press, 1979.

Joesting, Edward. *Hawaii: An Uncommon History.* New York: Norton, 1972.

Macpherson, Cluny, ed. *New Neighbors . . . Islanders in Adaptation.* Santa Cruz: Center for South Pacific Studies, University of California, 1978.

Oliver, Douglas L. *The Pacific Islands.* Cambridge: Harvard University Press, 1961.

Trumbull, Robert. *Tin Roofs & Palm Trees: A Report on the New South Seas.* Seattle: University of Washington Press, 1977.

INDEX

PICTURE CREDITS

DOUGLAS FORD is a New York–based writer who lived in Hawaii for two years. He received degrees in psychology and philosophy from the State University of New York at Stony Brook.

DANIEL PATRICK MOYNIHAN is the senior United States senator from New York. He is also the only person in American history to serve in the cabinets or subcabinets of four successive presidents—Kennedy, Johnson, Nixon, and Ford. Formerly a professor of government at Harvard University, he has written and edited many books, including *Beyond the Melting Pot, Ethnicity: Theory and Experience* (both with Nathan Glazer), *Loyalties,* and *Family and Nation.*